Woodworm

First published 2018 by The Hedgehog Poetry Press

Published in the UK by
The Hedgehog Poetry Press
Coppack House, 5
Churchill Avenue
Clevedon
BS21 6QW

www.hedgehogpress.co.uk

ISBN: 978-1-916480-62-9

9 8 7 6 5 4 3 2 1

A CIP Catalogue record for this book is available from the British Library.

Woodworm

by
Matt Duggan

Section 1:

Section 2

Acknowledgments

I would like to thank Mark the editor at Hedgehog Press for his support, patience, and for making Woodworm a reality. I'd also like to thank the following people that have inspired and brought light and life into my eyes my late grandparents Iris and Jack, my Mum and Dad Heather and Arthur, my partner Kelly Thomas, also like to thank the dreamers, poets, writers, survivors, agitators, editors, bar staff, artists, and subversives that I've had the pleasure of meeting over the last five years or so, plus a special dedication to a good friend and poet D.G. Geig and to thank him for his support, advice and kindness.
Black and White Author Artwork –
Pascale Gouverneur - Poet and Artist

Colour Artwork Images -
Kelly Thomas – Artist

Parkside Lounge Print - New York 2018
Crack in Reality – Philadelphia 2018

Part One

The Pursuit for Truth

In a Future We Didn't Expect

THE CITADEL

Metal spikes made from blue glass and silver
are unhooked – pierced inside shop entrances when closed
like dystopian fly- traps laid out to deter the homeless;

Shopping mall and arcade are pitched and layered
in stolen quilts, tents, and corners of toy cardboard
where between thin cracks the elevator rests.
A dead blues singer - her rasping tones
filter through corners like light on flash white algae;
Towers in settler red and gold paint a self-portrait of this city,
finger prints are used to milk tongues in clear digital chloroform.

Outside the diner I see an angel of disparity
walking in green squares - her eyes are like a mad bear chained at
a circus;
A sign attached around her head that reads...

'No WIFI, Just Smiles and Good Conversation.......'

A Starbucks beaker swirls in the bleached sun shining of dimes and quarters
where bodies are armed with designer shoes that step over empty cat litter
trays;
I look onto a world as a stranger in a very familiar and unequal land -
Enforcement officers dressed in lap-top black - eat chilli-dogs
monitor the latest headcount at Camp Hooverville;
Now let's move them on - make more space at the Citadel.

REVOLUTION

We are crab claws bones scattered on the sand
washed up from the beach returned to the master of sea;

Detached by the beauty that resonates from the deepest
surface of ocean. Where they throw us back onto dryland
believing that they can give just enough of what we want –

a veneer like salt to lassitude and distraction.
Though the sea is not our ruler who scribes out the future –

They ask that the revolution will never raise a glass to those comrades
as they've given us just enough of what we want -
no longer do we think for ourselves when we're mainlined into *google chrome.*

IN THE GARDEN OF SPRING

In the afternoon garden
full with flaws and clowns,
sipping apples with an ear
inside the bragging crowd;
an accent jumps like a bad audition
for a villain's bit part -
Streetwise Mockney
Into Afrikaans -
potato skins
in tarragon and paprika;
bearded men carry their spawn
inside beige papooses.
Ramblers gather
for latte
cappuccino
undermining whoever serves them!
Cocaine noses twitching
like tadpoles in a pool of teenage spittle,
I see them strutting,
swaying like hard shouldered drugstores;
Another afternoon
with the flaws and clowns of Spring.

QUESTIONING THE SPACE BETWEEN DRONES

Answers we seek are sometimes hidden
beneath the skin of wood and soil –
we must reveal ourselves to the world a little
before we can question the future and past;

Though this journey will bring hope and madness
in mirrors that won't reflect the true version of the self,

we must scale the battlements of our deepest
convictions; control the truth before the truth
simulates us. Dare the wind of spying drones
catch our shadow now citizens are suspected thieves;

let the rainbow blind the path of buzzing eye-lids
where lies are doctored in black and white screens;
Now confusion is the weapon of choice
hysteria – the oxygen they spread with outrageous spite;

We once believed our voices could make a change
though the frightened ones convinced the many
that everything remains the same.

THE TRANSFORMATION OF SEBASTIAN GILMOUR

Sebastian holds a plastic beaker of a well- known coffee corporation
(*that doesn't pay any tax*) shouts abuse at burger vans - hot-dog stands
wearing two Texan Longhorns on his feet; Banned all the meat eaters
from his favourite vegan restaurant. Unfortunate –
That they were a large percentage of its client base
(now no one can be bothered to go back in.)

Funding his life through his family trust fund
his Father was an original hippy from the sixties
who got rich from off shore real estate deals –
becoming the very first Yuppie of the 1980's;

Now Sebastian has grown blonde dreadlocks that smell of petiole -
tattooed a celtic band with the inscription MK ULTRA
on the end of his penis; Rejecting all the modern trappings of a material world
(apart from the latest updates from Apple)
soon the transformation appeared. Combats and fleece became a sharp blue
suit
trading in stocks and shares; the hair will be straightened –
dyed black- His car the most expensive and top of the range;

Sebastian holds a plastic beaker of a well- known coffee corporation
(*That doesn't pay any tax*) he no longer publicly shares his vexations
since he joined the largest legal crime syndicate in the world.

TENDERNESS

Drop a heart into a glass
watch the glass start to expand
place a lid or plate over its circular top;

Hear the slowing beat pulsate
allow oxygen to circulate. The heart
will become an unripe cacti fresh and cold,

bulging in liquid with hairs and horns
a tenderness revealed to all.

Show us that the moon is broken
peel away the broken glass
from the light that shatters;

Place the brightness inside
where the repletion of the dark
limps like a broken smile laid to rest.

Show me the sunset not the mouth
covering the concrete owl. The heart
that lay in tenderness waits to escape.

WHEN FOXES COME OUT TO PLAY

I rise before the dew
when the snails and crickets
race to the side- lines of the back garden;

Where stale pieces of tandoori chicken
plastic rind are resting on a party plate for the foxes –
I watch the night turn into day and my eyes turn
into giant blue turtle lights;

I watch them play in the opposite garden
The lawn is measured and cut to exact perfection;
As I see him watering his land for hours into days.

When the foxes come out to play – on his immaculate green
wrestling and biting digging up his perfectly lined pitch.

I should do the neighbourly thing
disturb them from their playing but it's so beautiful to see
fox cubs having so much fun – rolling in the amber sun playing as they
should.

DETRITUS

A busy waterfront – saffron coat of drunken leviathans, a crowd of silvery whores camp playboys waltzing with the lights from a lost traffic cone; They drink the warm whispers from cold women sipping from the immortal glass and its deathly charms that scribe in ink shades with shaking hands; Scoffing on *winter- berry* and *prosecco* hand cooked crisps where brave words ravish a lecher of mockery; Tongues leak the leftovers of politics pristine table tops with fragranced yellow candles laminated menu with marmalade steak; A collection of the graceful and grotesque littered streets of fish and chip bellies beggars stroll in suits and expensive casual dress. Behind the ruins in amber and elephant grey we hooked up dead celebrities in the abattoir stood in a matchbox of a black and white sunrise killing all the hippies turning their bones into gasoline; Wrapped in burger relish with too much cocaine a girl in high boots of leather steps over the wobbling wrecks of detritus; like fleshy relics in gutters mascara trails like dried lines of cold tar those portly creatures disperse for a brawl broken hair slides – ripped blouses at dawn. Those men that eat quinoa oatmeal a strawberry infused cappuccino with a short scattering of hazelnut were the men we knew as children who once fought imaginary witches on the high-street now they've succumbed to be the people who live inside hibernating in closed rooms as serial petition signers.

EVANESCED

Watching a *Kingfisher* puncturing surface –
a slewed flicker of blue diving through watery brown curtains;
Those moments submerged falling through another world
where time is slow and heavy;

the brief and lost scenes are a vivid retreat –
Where each abyss we visit the sweet chorus
listened for a fleeting white wren that will guide us;

If wanting to be far never caught by human eye;
like those missing moments when I drowned as a boy
thick reeds pulling me under;

a ship of small flames came waiting for me to ignite it –
leading the navigator into a new world that I may watch and cower –
Always be the ship mast not the sails;

Swim underneath the wreck be not that lifeless body
that floats on the surface; rooting wood where worms like to sleep;
Think and act as every eye would;

Be that watchful *Kingfisher* puncturing surface -
a slewed flicker of blue.

A WARNING

Bell chimes across the village and long valley
Green squares in identical formations –
Along walls of new architecture
they carve locust shells onto tombs without faces;
though we warn our children of the storm
that breathes openly in the gaps of history;

when flesh of war feeds the swarms of wingless nymphs
once from the Book of Exodus and plague of Capua
we ignored the world that paced up and down the hallway
distracted by plastic soldiers in a crimson moon
those denying apprentices of Auschwitz;

If they take a life in the name of the divine
they merely taste the wine that the devil squeezed
from the rib cage of poisoned Eve;

when the locusts have destroyed statues
antiquities of the past – we keep our heads lost in the forest
fascism is becoming trendy – human blood its serotonin;
How have we given the storm the repetition that it needs?.

MIDNIGHT IN NEW YORK

I'm not wiping sweat from my forehead
but cobwebs from the metal ferns;
I appear to be drunk on 23rd street
having forgot the name of my hotel again;

I see the scaffolds around famous Chelsea
Her velvet claws are sticking out
like the hotels sharpened teeth dripping blood
onto the fire hydrants and the busy streets below;

I talk with bar-men who speak with two accents
yellow cabs pierce tall smoky traffic queues
hear a city that never sleeps whisper to me
down blocks of red bricks and repetition of basket- ball parks

Smell of Cinnamon from a Deli drifting
next to an Irish pub cooking fresh chowder -
I breathe in the smell and break the chains of morning;
hear a city that never sleeps whisper to me, *it's time for bed.*

THE DIONYSIAN

We once lived in a den among thieves
spent afternoons sleeping in hammocks
smoking the rarest imported sativa;

(Where are all of those Dionysian's now?)

The boys that I'd once shared different worlds with -
when the sky was the colour of harvesting salt lakes;
I suppose we might of taken it to the edge of all edges
ending up on day release tending and watering bright flowers
in the most colourful of hospitals in town; swapping illuminating
dreams for a tablet box full of fiction.

Instead we drank ourselves into a mild sedation
watched other people live their lives on a large screen;
We said goodnight to another world's notifications
stretch out our ego's so everyone could see.

THE FUTURE ISN'T WHAT WE EXPECTED

Seek pastures in olive beneath a bitter moon that twists the space between day and twilight; Realise with each passing decade we exist to dismember our own past. We look up the dress of Lady Liberty turquoise stockings glowing in sunlight - Searching for the fragments of balance is like catching the departure of a disappearing shadow. We were happy enough to chase our tails for a lifetime use our fingers to type our pelvic muscles to take selfies -placing the white noise to all human distractions a digital mask that highlights our decision making; We should of stolen the black honey from the hive of Prometheus but instead we walk in the spaces of rented out amnesia - Crimson sleepers snore while standing up in a city downloaded where citizens palm read and gutter gaze – constructed and vetted by a selection that has already processed you
(You are a low risk dissident – deemed safe – Non-confrontational)

If you are the man that chief ink blotter of state and corporate redactions would you blot out the wrong words? reveal the most relevant news embarrassing the brass at the top of the money tree? Send full encrypted memos detailing the expenses of our public representatives where evidently death would be added to the files with *Frank Olson;
(Censored - Letters blacked out - Digitally Removed)

These chains that we had lifted over our heads the iron shackles left inside the earth; dirty soil had unpicked the lost padlock interning the season of tomorrow into one; We only ever saw what was in front of us never searching behind the last elevation - We never went beyond our own viewpoint as the world is only what we see inside our rear view mirror.

---

*Frank Olson was a bacteriologist biological warfare scientist and CIA employee who worked at Camp Detrick(Now Fort Detrick) in Maryland, and was involved in the MK Ultra Experiments, he was covertly dosed with LSD by his CIA supervisors and plunged to his death from the window of a 13th storey New York City hotel room.

AUTUMN

It was between two September moons
that I saw her breath drift among the autumn debris
lightness of day wrapped on wet broadsheets

where I hear jostling winds like small children
playing in gardens of floating ship wrecks.
The morning as dark as star anise;

air shows cubes of rain falling under
spotlights waking from sleep.
Her summer eyes are lost in the dankness
that even the roses in the park look grey;

This season unlocks timid streams of sun and frost
onto the falling leaves that camouflage a young fox
gathering scraps from the remains of Sunday Tea;

Rarely do we see any light in the break of autumn
just that black and white celluloid glow
slowly preparing us for the cold stay of Winter.

THE HUNT

Twenty eight pairs of eyes
chase moving amber
over pockets of broken snow;

I always believed that sport was supposed
to be gauged by two equals;
for strength and agility not an army verses one.

The men that ride in red through winter streams
corked by the sun are the emblematic reasons
why I retreat from any form of patriotism.

They harness the empirical nature of a darkness that lingers
in the cygneous cracks of a country's neck;
that once spread into its lungs to voice privilege and class division;

Twenty eight pairs of eyes chase moving amber -
over pockets of broken snow.

INSIDE THE REMAINS OF STOKE PARK COLONY

I walk as a child with my Mother
over buttercup mounds to a verge in Purdown;
paddle in the water at Duchess Gate
above a land covered in oak and lady birds.
Watched a stranger in a window with white bars
heard sounds of a horse running and only ever felt his breath –
some have said it's the grey lady riding–
the ghost of *Elizabeth Somerset. One late summer's afternoon;

they unlocked large chrome padlocks –
dandelions interwoven as large silver chains.
we walked around the hallway of The Dower House –
Beside broken E-C-T trollies a crumbling staircase
collapsed prison-cells that held what the state determined then
as the feeble minded gene pool; I heard a horse
drinking from his trough but never got to see the horse;
three knocks at the obelisk they say – Elizabeth may show her face.

*In 1790 a 17 year old girl called Elizabeth Somerset fell off her horse and broke her neck in the grounds of The Dower House in Stapleton, Bristol. It is said that her ghost continues to ride around the grounds, also known to some as The Grey Lady. I worked as a Nursing Assistant at Stoke Park Hospital from 1990- to its closure in 1994, and I and several others got to look around inside the Dower for a few hours on the last day before the Hospital closed for good. Both my Mum and my Nan Iris also worked at some time in their careers in psychiatric care.

INSERT HUMAN EXPLETIVE

If the coast is calm
ink of cloud splayed
hill of clay and sand
delve on banks spliced;
In plastic mutations
sculptured by animal feet
legs in unskinned red fur
unearthed bottled fins
mountain and scattered shore
radioactive dinner plate
snout in woodchip and stout;
Thin bones of insects
float inside dead grey buds
where oxygen is shared
between thirsty reptiles;
Whose eggs are hatched
inside the fluorescent
blue tubes of sunbeds.

TREE

A man takes a photograph of a tree- heart
carved with a pen- knife by an innocent hand
an arrow is chipped in bark -spear head much darker
than any winter's night; Initials immortalized in oak.
Do tree hearts ever fade in time and if so
are they replaced by their latest love?

If time let the heart dissolve into the root
will initials ever change or remain the same?
Those not so innocent hands are now covered
yellow beer and the usual Friday night insults;
Would they ever notice their young inscription
inscribed upon the chest of the very same ageing tree.

THE IRON CHILDREN

My grandfather like Jesus used his hands on wood –
worked at Parnell's factory in a palace of red splinters,
"The Lady should be burning not turning" he shouted
while standing with his hands like fleshed red sinter;

We finished at the Gateway on Saturday and took acid tabs –
(usually Purple Ohms) Jumped off the local park benches
to feel the sky rise from the ground; We bought singular cigarettes
and had our first pints at the Greyhound at sixteen

       (which cost 64 pence).

We, the iron children- a relic of coal and steel
the sticky blood of mines once discarded;
our eyes the burning tin from drowning mountains
where schools and hearts were eaten up by strikes and drilling giants.
When I read Kafka, Verlaine, Harrison,

....and Sue Townsend –

(Adrian Mole was all the rage -
And so was that bloody Thatcher).

NEW BEGINNING

We watched a man chase rainbows off the estate
starched pattern circled his greased back hair
sipping a boiler maker with a brandy chaser -
a glass of Cherry B for the wife.

We were immortals in the garden of cement
packed bullet shells inside our duffle coats
ran from yellow and green darts of hay-fever
that had chased us over crow prowling quarries;
where glue bags stuck to climbing frames
like luminous lights glowing inside a cathedral;

We stumbled through chalk white dog- excrement
arriving home before our nighty clout,
we never questioned the ways things were;
How the screams every Friday night next door got louder!

AN INTRODUCTION TO THE ENGLISH CLASS SYSTEM

Introduced to the horrors of priggishness
when I met some boys who attended a local school

(Not dissimilar to Hogwarts)

I'd imagined them playing chess- sipping lavender tea
plotting how they were going to destroy the working class.
I know some who idolise with such envy -
severing arteries for a handful of what they've got

the brutal ones laughed at the sweat on our hands
grunting in dark sarcasm in secret wooden rooms;
as we destroyed personalities in a square tablet prison
described to us as a prestigious social retreat -

those working class heroes that we once knew
swapped gourmet burgers for Foe Gras in saffron,
ascending into a world that they couldn't afford
becoming everything that they once despised.

THE PLIGHT OF THE WORKING-CLASS

I.

Filling up on mud coffee one lunch time
a worker put down his newspaper.
He saw through the print into an unheard lie -

deciding to no longer dance that dance with them;
imposters had embellished the falsehoods of his self
yet they followed them like a squadron of rats in rhythm and time;

When a worker put down his newspaper
doesn't believe what he reads anymore –

He'll follow that realisation by trying to down
all of his work tools. A worker is then labelled a shirker,
a commie, a conspiracy nut, then quickly alienated
from his work colleagues - Then subtle belittled until he finally quits;

A worker picks back up his newspaper
keeps his views very much to himself ,
sealed and locked sentences behind self - censored lips.

II.

Around him stand people
he once thought of as brethren

They switched their personalities
with their social standing; ignoring those
who earned well below them.

A worker sits at the bar hiding his expletives
under a gingham dressed basket of triple cooked chips;
His work colleagues are now very different strangers
that he feels it's like drinking salt with fat sweaty slugs

(who were once wild and free butterflies)

Their words are slim and selfish and every sentence
spins a new theory for self -marketing their management skills;
How empty is their cup that will never be filled
with any of the true essentials needed for a well contented friendship .

ORATOR OF PETERLOO

The Orator travelled the length of the land through bare corn field to busy city- street; kicking sand into the face of the landowner - *Repel these laws of mercantilism and allow small and broken mouths to feed and eat*; Do not let this highly taxed trade be our prison. Wavering poles topped with the red cap of liberty the ear of a nation gathered to listen to a man who wants to blind the parliamentary horse giving every man and woman the right -a voice - not lost inside a crowd; the vision of an eye that directs the governments sight. The Orator saw bones in red mud a shrill from daughter to mother; fists and shrugs of the disempowered stealing breadcrumbs from their neighbours; the banners held high read of *REFORM, EQUAL REPRESENTATION, and LOVE.* Words delivered that day echo how we all feel as we heard the sound of long blades withdrawing - the Hussars approached on horseback preparing for the final charge; murdering children, men, and women as the Orator words could not stop the unfolding of this bloody mindless slaughter.

THE LEY

As a small boy I climbed onto an American Tank
in peat coloured black. Bark from castles made from gun turrets –
submerged in cliffs of emerald blue;

the thin shingle and smell of ocean
lingers between the skin of the ley
like a road held in an angel's tempting grips;
Simmering of river and sea grew closer with time.

Fishing nets snagged in grey metallic whale
as ghosts of algae summoned a water god -
made the land a finger of white sand
covered with reeds in yellow and dusty green -

The storm can break the road that holds
the Kingfisher's back from sea;
When the ley floods with salt, wave, and sand;

The river will become blue where butterflies once flew
in air puddles of pollen – seahorses drowning
in the shallow mix like two seasons combining poison into one.

HAVE YOU EVER SEEN ANGELS PLAYING AN EVENING OF GRAVE-HOPPING?

If we don't see the death maiden of conflict
filling our curved widescreens with blood
– then – it will ease from memory
replaced with glitter, pomp, trooping of the colour;
Let us not ask *Google* today or type while walking into lampposts;
Scrolling on bus stops and peeping into other people's lives.

(In these rooms of amnesia we watched red and grey offices
lighting up; saw the luminous murals depicting
our inner disillusions in comedic and satirized characters;)

We passed disused multi-coloured trams sleeping
in waste of black confetti; Pinstripe trees ensemble
like tall dark knights of order angels play
an evening of grave-hopping while a fox is pissing
in the air drunk on the dregs from a dirty drip trays;

Traffic is slow. Engine fumes move like chalk
slammed against a blackboard; Breath is tightening. Chest grinds.
Ribcage aches our anxiety is a cage; City of grey death – tubes of windows
on giant stilts peer down on tiny shadows; where panic is building a home
inside eyes of newspapers. Moving billboards reveal a life that doesn't exist.
We take refuge in Parkland at lunchtime – an Eden among a city of stars
that spits out neon effigies; small pockets of earthly heaven
make us calmly breath again among whispering oak and talkative seagulls.

YGGDRASIL

Eight of nine branches severed
our tree of life span nine worlds in all.
land of blue lavender field of white heather;
heaven rejected the dead root
where the dragon of *Nifiheim*
once chewed on green ash and oak;
Bones are now the leaves
in an eagle's nest where only a thread remains.

Our absolute truth hangs
inside the hollow gut of a dying tree;
We hold the woodman's heavy axe
in one hand - lung of the world in the other;
sharpening the blunt silver blade
squeezing the air for atmosphere
playing god for a brief moment
our claws hang on the last weakened thread.

COFFEE AND REVOLUTION

It was Avicenna a Persian opium fiend
who first told us stories about the pleasure of coffee.
How it grew wild and free on the Arabian peninsula
those oil-rich berries mixed with fat and alcohol;
The hot black water from warmed Syria
could sterilize nature and extinguish carnal desire,
drank once only by clergy and aristocracy.
We have not banned tea and coffee breaks as yet
(the only legal drug ritual left to us,
now they've banned us from smoking cigarettes)
It is said "if wild talk be the mother of revolution
then coffee houses must be its midwife"
if so, social media must be the after pill;
the mainstream newspapers the father to all of its delusions.

THE GIRL FROM PATITIRI

Slicing tuna skins pickling eyes in ouzo –
comb of Kalamata olives; cubes of feta
resembled plastic dice without any spots.
The girl from *Patitiri* carried buckets of water
on the back of a mule through villages
in nectarine and sea hawk green.

She kept a dozen black kittens
left black flowers on the garden's wooden
chest for Poseidon; Suckled a god's blood
from a rectangle obelisk smelt fresh pine
with madness and mint. She hung a red dress
over the hollow guts of a olive tree
collected the island's souls that would wander -
leading them to prayer on the smallest chapel
on sleepy *Patitiri,* its cross coloured
like the shine of fresh *Melitzana.*

We question is the girl really the Goddess Adicia ?
this girl who sliced tuna skins and pickled eyes in ouzo!
I saw her in town today sipping a chilled Retsina
while she danced sensually to the sound of Cuba.

UNDER THE MOON AND BENEATH THE EARTH

Under the moon and beneath the earth
we see the jittering coast line the stars no longer hide
Behind veils of dark tubes our voices move towards
the moon's time-dial; That once kind stranger

Stands on the edge of a river bouncing stones
against the duck oak tree inscribed with painted
white love hearts; That you once craved
into its pale flesh with a butterfly red coloured penknife.

Bodies face the circular yellow god
our eyes formed breaths that started to breathe;

Yesterday the walls had ears that listened to us
today our fingerprints leave a continued trace;
Even when beneath this earth the soul will not grow tired
until that house of ill and infamy lay in flames, ash, and rubble.

LAMENT

Don't replace the same armour where open wounds
are healed by breath not medicine; Take an orchid as soft as a pillow
sleep in the secret garden among fresh opiates;

Rest well my friend where the sun hacks the rainbow into quarters;
Catch the thief who unthreads such old wounds – Please do leave
those promises at the door as time will heal all of the spaces that are left
behind.

I heard you read in an armoury in Massachusetts
we shared a smoke outside along avenues of painted white wood
Picket fences and square porches; We discussed the eternal
those elements of inertia over drinks and nachos;

Rest well my friend where the sun hacks the rainbow into quarters;
leave the light to burn until the smell of gasoline no longer lingers,
wave goodbye to the road that was once broken and disjointed;
Sleep well my friend and may the guardians hold and guide you.

For D.G.Geis

Part Two

Questioning Sanity
In A Post- Truth Age

LOOK WHAT WE'VE BECOME

Land of neo brown shirts – white cliffs
a strict border layered in red brickwork,
fishing boats once saviours for the persecuted.
We now build walls from those we've liberated;

Cut off our own ears awakening a poisonous serpent for oil,
dormant inside Persian sands; which resurrected
the buried voices in charcoal.

Dusting jackboots are stomping on gravestones of our ancestors
though we'd fill a whole lake with blood oil
we starve our children leaving them on its banks.

We cut out our hearts from empathy
as repetitive nights of Kristallnacht returned.
No longer do we recognise our enemy
taking sides for the highest price

our isolated island - a ghost ship with no sails
our captain unsure of our destination,
stirring us into unknown waters
towards an economic tsunami;

Land of neo brown shirts – white cliffs
a strict border layered with red brickwork.

SEPARATION

Did you hear the voice from inside a doll's house?
It was left outside next doors front gate with a porcelain figure
abandoned from their loved ones - taken away
inside a white van- with chipped furniture – grey broken slate.
They once played inside a garden full of space and sun
now the grass is long and only dead sunflowers in a vase remain;
It was during the summer that they all had to walk away -
the wife carried the balloons as her daughter walked behind;

A bridge of trust between them had been split in two
they lived in separate rooms searching for a better future;
The daughter travelled the earth for the voices inside her doll's house -
believing the answers to separation could be found somewhere inside;
Listening out attentively for that familiar voice from childhood
she had carried the key - determined to unlock their sadness one day
a visit to a second hand toy shop - Busy Sunday markets -
where hope is a child's voice locked inside a cardboard hallway.

A POEM FOR THOMAS (A LETTER FROM THE KING)

He'd always shoot the cowboys
in those black and white westerns
with the long barrel of his walking stick;
I only ever heard the war stories
when I got much older –
how he saved a new recruit –
by pulling a bullet out of the back of his neck;
That young boy is now a retired clerk;
Who visits us with presents twice a year
where the medals, letter from the King are taken
from a drawer for the very last time.
Red woollen blanket warms my Grandfather's shrapnel leg
a quarter moon of wispy and whitened hair –
oak like wrinkled tan of dark bronze;
On the coffee table a green book rests
(The history and conflict of Mesopotamia)
inside the inner pages - a dozen thin and crispy maps
detailing his bloodied siege at *Kut- Al- Amara;

*Poem written for my Grandfather Thomas Duggan who fought at the Great Siege of Kut-Al-
Amara in 1915 and survived, during the six month siege located in today's Iraq, British troops
experienced starvation, lack of ammunition and disease, all of which led to surrender in April
1916. Thousands of troops were sent to Mesopotamia now modern day Iraq, following the late
Ottoman Empire's entry into the war in 1914. Britain was desperate to protect its oil supplies in
the region. Thomas returned to Bristol in the U.K. and lived with his relatives and sons until he
was well into his 80's.

THE CROOKED TREE

Between the gaps in the crooks
light in resin amber and silver- grey shine
I catch the brief moments of happiness
the oneness and the carnal world unleashed;
I'll meet you under the crooked tree
When the stars are fenced from view
see the mists cover the laundry field
where mass hospital bedsheets once dried;
now those plastic wards are all closed
lunatics stroll around the perimeters
in dew and in dusk in night and in day;
counting cigarette ends with a gutter gaze
for hearts once torn can now share the light hidden
underneath the crooked tree where we closed and listened.

DIETING ADVICE FOR ARTEMIS*

After all the years of hunting boar
and having barbecues in the forest
Artemis is worried about her high blood pressure
We suggested that she seek a dieting alternative
maybe lay off the Atkins diet and try out a week of veganism;
She's now traded in her horse for a treadmill on e-bay
swapped her golden crossbow for a gym membership with Orion;
except on every other Saturday –

(When she treats herself to a large glass of Malbec
with a fillet of medium rare - juicy Argentinian).

EATING MYTHS IN B-MINOR

Riding mechanical wings
dolphins swerve like white sails
Flat roofs in Moorish amber;
Hooves of *Pegasus* are cooked
charcoaled with baby onions and raisins
in a Taverna named B-minor;
Situated between the sleepy town of Hora
and the first steps to Olympus.
Twist a mountain from view
smell the fresh pine inhaled –
hear a sunset gather dust and dew;
cackles of ash - burning on a stove.

Mix red currents minted juniper
wings of a *Moth Man* removed
diced and marinated – 28 day cured
West Virginia meat moulded into small patties
cooked slowly over a medium heat.
Feast comes every Sunday
a fresh slice of the Goddess of *Pulque*
where 400 simmering Aztec breasts are soaked
in maguey sap; a slowly cooked dish aptly named
(Centzon Totochtin)
But do be warned as we've been told
that soon we'll be as drunk as 400 rabbit gods.

WHEN WINTER BRINGS ME MY SICKNESS

When the smell of Lavender
no longer drifts in the garden
pavements are orange and matted –
carpet of dead leaves.
Sky loses its vibrant colours
as winter begins to breathe
moored in skylines that bleed snow;
where I feel that winter will bring me my sickness;
On days where moods like to hide
in the spaces of silver breaths,
wait like an expectant bride
beneath ashes of unnecessary confetti.
When winter brings me my sickness –
I'll sleep with the bones of isolation
naked under the flickering candlestick,
a muted and self-exiled alienation.

THE SHAPE OF BROKEN

It was a hot summer when bark peeled from the trees
pavements - looked like they were obstructed
by the shattered debris of tortoise shells;

I walked through steep lanes where several men slept in the shadows –
the ground was cooling above a sky in the shape of broken;
Trees had shed their skin - vulnerable to the ailment of earth
flesh is the shaven white oak – opening arms to the worms and the rain;
How baring the core of the self may join shapes together -
crowded and misplaced and peeled away layers of skin;

Allowing the weak and fragile mask to feed
those snapping bones of the actors that came and died;
Spurious grins that split bark on a stage - that peeled away from the tree.

SWIMMING AMONG JAGGED ROCKS

If I'm the last remains of cliff face
You surely must be the sea
Finger-tips are the rocks
That lay beneath my feet;
Though the birds still sing
Autumn leaves fall
more elegantly with age
I'll hang here some more
occasionally immersing my toes
in the envelope of salt
that soaks my skin with such rage;
When I'm worn and broken
a chipped footpath eroding
clumps of land balancing sun shadows
across a bay of jagged rocks;
I fear not the cuts and breakage of the flight/fall
It's what I can't see beneath the surface
that has me suspended between two worlds.

DISCARDED SONNETS FOUND INSIDE A FORD CORTINA

I suppose she never read them
bundled up in a W.H Smiths shopping bag –
hidden inside the dashboard of a Ford Cortina
Did those lustful dreams of her shine through?
young heart strapped in seats of disposable angst;
Sometimes the dream you want never fulfils the reality
when you do kiss what you should have been kissing
those young sonnets of longing and desire
are brought back to life for a brief moment;
we held each other tightly while friends
avert their eyes at time catching up with its ghosts
a love that had finally found its rightful home;
even if it was only for a short and brief vacation
where words once written will never be discarded again.

WALKING WITH COLERIDGE IN CLEVEDON *

On the day the first snow- flakes fell
along a muddied jigsaw shore,
slim boats lined with black blushed tails
smeared grit on brown labyrinth floor.
Path of tobacco and crosses in dead oak
matted with feathers and yellow moss
on waters where lost epiphanies float
above the slewed ringlets in polished frost.

I saw the painting of that man from Ottery
following him along the small palms of frozen sand,
beneath a jacinth coloured moon this wreckage of moonlight –
a circled sinew of bloated white rain.
Vinegar trails in a child's frosty hands
like lines of wax embalmed into cemented snow,
grass verge is a train track rustic and twinned
where a balaclava covered chip-fryer is shivering.

Close to a distant pier with green shining railings
a charred black orchid casted out at sea
vast cloudless sky sailing in dark colours
that can only hear an ocean stopping to breathe.
Car engine coughing among the mists of warming sleet
like fish-hooks that sway in dull twilight;
Winters canvas swallowing pin pricks of zenith light,
that shined on the children playing hopscotch on broken glass.

*Highly Commended and runner up in the Road to Clevedon Pier Competition

PREDICTABLE

We've not heard from him his presence has become quiet;
Still hear his whisper – when eyes were watering yet no one was crying;
Will he return – Sit among them again?

Carry inspiration for others
guide them to the places
that they've only ever dreamed about;

It was him- they manipulated –
Used him to see how far they could push him;
slander his advice

while ostracizing him for his own success;
like an ancient statue
they created cracks underneath his flesh –

The predictable circle revealed themselves
leaving him alone on Robinson's bench
without even a thank you note.

That's why we've not heard from him;
Why his presence no longer sits at the table with them;
he is gone – pushed away – (like Chatterton without arsenic).

THE DUNES

We watched the sea shells dragged
as rain signalled for hope.
It was close to the dunes
when I kissed her;
Under a picture of a chapel
Yet behind her wild stare
smeared make-up,
underneath the spiked
blonde hair – a scream was silenced
by a dirty secret that only her father would know.
How would I have reacted?
if I knew the secret of which I know now.

DID YOU SEE THE GHOST OF KHASOGGI WEARING A FAKE BEARD?

This fabled bloodline that pierced young hearts
why do we help plough burnt land and city?
recycling dangerous metals –
rivers of sarin and yellow chlorine.

Hold a silver calibre to the base of our toes
feed on the sorrow that we brought upon ourselves
We pride our western freedoms, values, choice and civility
holding palms with our children's executioner;

We slept with the black bloodied hydra
impregnating its philosophy into one thousand
new snake babies - so much innocence we slay
tongue of future promise morality hides under beaten floorboards

where a clock is paused suckled on the strings that pull
the darkened heart of Wahhabism,
should we not re-evaluate our relationship?
when the Sword of Saud cuts the throats of criticism

We continue to bow and give hot dangerous metals
supply a new brigade with a dead man's box of medals
place a sweet moreish chocolate in one palm
cut the other with disabling toxins;

Those decisions to economise from the scraps of war
the taunt of new oil and family bloodlines gorged -
we sold the golden trigger and created our own madness
keeping the world's river running in a violent shade of red.

HE HUNGER

ll that's left are the berry pickers
e foxes have gone – magpies have flown far from the storm;
'e watched children throwing stones at drones
at hovered above council estates,

'aiting for that interlude – the lightness –
symphony we can't hear. Stomach is brimming
ht muscles can't clench wilderness not reached –

'e draw this hunger in pencil across a sky in dark velvet;
lk among dunes of concrete where fumes fill a green arena;

ur sanity disturbs this restless hunger as we devour colours and textures
cking images that tempt our throats; waiting for that interlude – the lightness – the break.

AN AMERICAN BREAKFAST

After returning to the subtle sound of traffic
I reflected on journeys from cradle of liberty
to the widening crack in Liberty Bell;

I drank a straw of Bukowski's Blood
in a velvet bar full of rain; Fed myself up on cheesesteaks
suckle on the dew from an ancient *Oyster Bis,*
(made from the freshest of fish brains.)

I ate waffles with cream and jalapeno for breakfast
then watched the *Citgo* sign of Boston switch back on -
where *Duke* and *Billie Holiday* once sang and performed.
Skin floats between chrome towers a stub of fresh blood;

Vampires on Wall Street step over sleeping bodies
like dried cum stains on bathroom floors -
Flesh is cold and some are still warm and twitching.

THE CORPULENCE OF ATHENA

Smoking the last cigarette in the pack
Athena flicks through the Daily Mail;
she unblocks her hotel room of empty pizza boxes
stacked up like snared and ripped dominoes;
She's developed agoraphobic tendencies
a fondness for waffles chocolate buttons and cream;
dependency to feed her sugar addicted brain.
Reason, logic, and morality were gifts
only given to gods as mortals never
listened to wisdom, instead they took
her knowledge and used it like it was their own;
She had called this the plagiarism of man –
refusing his manipulated acuity;
She exiled herself into a hotel room for a feast of *fast food*,
inertia, and self- proclaimed *obscurity.*

WE SEE THE DUST BEFORE IT BECOMES THE LIGHT

Admiring the old cash registers
that line many of the bars –
gaunt silver brown with rusted head
keys are like large circles of metallic coins;
They remind me of the old Remington typewriters
a huge mass of metal that sparkles
every time it rings; Through a small alley
where a terrier sits in the window
his face such sad eyes forming warm tears.
Breath is glistening on translucent squares;
Gazing at the air outside and the children
that doodle smiley faces on steamy glass.

We see the dust before it becomes the light.
My sanctity is the shape of wooden spokes
when the heart only cared to fall upwards and sideways;
the world that I knew beneath my growing feet
is a land of storm-troopers and dead glue-sniffers;
That time is with us now no matter which mask
you decide to go and hide behind; Truth is the imperative
choice for our kind as we are being systemically crushed
like shipyard prawns at dusk; Counting the ticking clock
between lucid dreaming; the night holds the candle
as we tread the moments keeping the memory alive;
We see the dust before it becomes the light.

SOCIAL MEDIA

The boy had never heard of telephone boxes
never tried talking with real girls in the flesh -
only the glamourous sex bots online
over sweaty qwerty white keyboards;

Where socialising in total isolation
once trickled to us as having sociopathic tendencies;
The boy made up of broken up shards -

(Only fights his battles on Social Media.)

She looks deep into her screen polishing up her profile
extra glitter and glam; I, am Instagram she declares
scrolling through all of her enemies and trolls;

missing out on a world that is slowly falling apart.
Her God's are algorithms and selfie sticks
she looks up from her phone into a world where nothing else remains

(Except her. Realising that the more she used Social Media
the more anti- social she became.)

LOVE AND CINEMA

Colour of her face changed when the moon draw obsidian shapes
across her skin; head outlined in oval like a pencil sketch made without any
paper.
Could she scream and feel the convulsion of lights inside of her?

That impossible inclination that love was an imaginary scene –
audio textures taken from a film; She closed her tin box of bitter resentments-
placed them inside her embroidered yellow pockets for an hour

She only ever came alive when the darkness filled the auditorium ;
When impenetrable light was banished to the foyer; It was only then
that she could watch herself falling in love all over again.

GLOBALISATION

When you own the world the mind that hosts
all of our endeavours truth becomes a prison
that in the end imprisons itself;

Through the eye of ink and mouth of stiff collars –
an exodus, where pinstripe heathens
clench their fists more pound and dollar.

I feel the fight is now falling from our fingers
lost in the same window display –
a season where all clouds are shaped
like sleeping dragon's; All the takeaway coffee
tastes exactly the same; What interests the pocket
to a marketing heathen those people
that dwell in posturing hallways rolling fifty
pound notes up on the thighs of politicians;

When you own the world truth becomes a prison
that in the end will imprison itself.

MAGPIE

We are distracted magpies made of skin and metal
slowly building our own prisons – brick by brick

absorbed inside the world of a small black case -
that wields our knowledge, status, and power.
We fly between truths a bird without a final destination;

our calling for the silver that detracts us is the lighting glint
a city more powerful than the empathy held inside our being;
We collect shiny obsolete silver objects replacing them every other year.

Our behaviour is engineered as is our desensitised response to a blood
soaked image – to immediately go out and buy more useless shiny goods -

We are distracted magpies made of skin and metal
slowly building our own prisons – brick by brick.

THE LIVING AND THE DEAD

I walk the same path into the city on the same day graffiti flaked on broken cemented hips houses lathered in bind weed and ivy -the moon patrols the earths circling lips on the day an island was losing its soul -the lion sipped milk from a fleshless carcass; We didn't smell the fresh bread anymore only chorizo and onion on wooden burnt sticks cheap glass of Prosecco – a silver bowl of Wasabi nuts; I could smell the lost and tattered drops of mint spinning in gardens like twisted shapes as the skinned dead walk the same popular spots; drained their eyes in paper cuts with last year's ink as the news recycles and only simulates the repetitions that all truth is sworn to the death of the living; Angels played roulette on the floors of God's abattoir and we saw mushroom spiralling like sun from coral – A leather of blue waves circling mannequins in paradise - an embryo of the fallout where hell was a grain of pacific sand where man strips away the flesh unwiring himself from the human looking glass, our eyes shine like achromatic pupils dripped in one voice; We kicked conker shells into soft glimmers of contaminated water where our reflections fluttered on the surface like dirty lavender far from the earth and it's dog star – Residing in a glass box where we can't feel; Through six shades of glass part of our world had stopped people were talking but we couldn't hear each other's words like the ghosts of friends behind screens who couldn't see us. As long as the glass doesn't crack we will believe anything while locked inside this glass box we have the world on button; All we know is where the paper trail ends - where the spiral staircase without a top floor leads.

FINDING EDEN

Swimming so far from the crowd to stronger waves
that guide me back to the shore -

I confess all of my sins to a theatre without any faces
where the only ears listening are the cracks in bathroom mirrors.
Autumn leaves fall like lotus eaters retrieving the dead
I'd found my Eden and never tasted the fruit -
as golden buds lay in sticky puddles of rust
among the remains of poached angel feathers;

A stranger wears the pierced armour of lost paradise
where all the delights had long ago expired and decayed
I'd found my Eden at last and never quite tasted the fruit,
formed in a man-made paradise now deranged and unhinged.

THE PLOT TO KILL WHAT COULD NEVER BE

I.

I didn't want to wear another coat made from secrets and shadows
the second layer of dust that wilts and doesn't exist;
a whisper only heard between very good friends.
Her smile cracked the ice that appeared in my drink
we both held love in a cup and drank from its very core;
her image remained with me like the breaking shade of day.
Never would I walk into her land again as the battlements from her King
would be reinforced – I'd be left to feel like I was Paris at the last days of Troy.

II.

I kept a polaroid of her hidden underneath half bitten toy soldiers and my
action man
she had kissed me down a hallway of electric white classrooms –
where toilet paper stuck to walls and slide down the cracks
into bathroom mirrors; She held my heart and squeezed it
until I couldn't breath – slowly peeled away the layers and spat out the pips.
I'd find the closure that I needed and the realisation that first loves are never
eternal;
though left alone it would only be lust that controlled us –
as the plot to kill what could and would never be was eventually realised.

LEARNING TO FLY

Wings clipped tied down by chain and length of sea
in a dream I found instruments to make me fly
no longer trying to bounce off walls and concrete trampolines,

(I'm learning to fly again.)

When the locks are broken –
cement unhinged I'll fly where the shadows bend
following the light that feeds me, along a path that I'm supposed to take

though the claws are far away reaching out from the land below,
where I can hear a slight murmur of voices
I'm learning to fly into this world again

You must ignore the distractions
the snide and snake like venom of character
that may attract you back to the least revealing challenge;

Rise above those that will only ever
pull on your heels like hungry termagants ;
make the journey beyond anyone's expectations of you;

After the pain has submerged you'll see how the void
will slowly make you fly where no one will pull at the heel
weigh you down by placing tassels of regret on those wings.
The Journey

Anecdotes of a life half -lived fuel in an empty engine
optimised by a silver headed match
that you carry inside my eyes waiting to ignite it –

lead the navigator into a new world
so I may watch you cower behind it –
Did I Piss on your *Psychopomp?*

Keeping me in the shadow so to break the light
that you use to punish me. Bring logic, surprise,
realism, and *truth* on the journey.

The elements of which have alluded
the sacrifice that people can't see;

Always keep dreams so close
those enemies far from you.
Be the ship mast not the sails

where underneath the shipwreck
the rooting wood reveals the worms that sleep
inside the last resting place on earth.

WOODWORM

Never would we see through the wood of truth hear the guarded secret of the murmuring worms; ashes of documents held in black vaults eye a pendulum of silenced voices. They dropped madness into a glass of water wanting to direct the arrows that pulled our strings -when you feed the mad even more madness only secrecy in locked rooms would remain; A guardian of secrets can kiss a fool in front of a god revealing to the cupbearer the midnight the sirens forgot to sing; Change the colour and texture of the sea for one day make fierce dragons come to life in twinned rooms with mirrors. We see the damage it's done on the surface never see inside or beneath the carnage it unleashed; The men with black hats who had fingers like camera straps distracted our focus from the main decisions of the day. Where our dollar and pound became the gold stitching in pockets with coins made from petroleum; Stitching unthreaded - the bare fields a black pocket left bare Replaced with the rattle of red bullets; the mantra to an economy of repetitive wars. We show you the daily prompts of ideological strategies - immersed in the dust that cakes the western lungs; you may catch the face that's hidden in the cracks of splintered wood.

BUTTERFLY

A butterfly never meets its mother
hardwired to travel to the same place –
condition without thinking
a transformation of its formal self;
The circle it travels a repetition of its birth
mould the pattern - no empathy or compassion;
the easy way to ply an incidental thought.
When a caterpillar dreamt of its flight
understand that an ending started at the beginning;
the symbol of a butterfly – holds the perfect moment in time
remembered briefly and then suddenly forgot.

ARMAGEDDON (PARTS I AND II)

I.

I'll stay in when world leaders start swinging their balls around.
The ground outside was a little damp
patch of grey with pockets of white –

No meteorologist report as yet.
The T.V. Fuzzy. Blank.
texture outside very similar to artificial sand.

Stay indoors on Wednesday
there's a likelihood of a heavy pouring of reaping
expect high gravitation a little ceiling creeping
lasting well into Friday – lay off *A- roads* and *motorway*

as angels will be purging late Tuesday with a high possibility
that Lucifer will arrive on Saturday
just in time for the last ever episode of *STRICTLY.*

II.

Let's FUCK for the last remaining seconds be inside each other's limbs
before we finally turn to dust. We can talk about the Abrahamic
religion's disputable origins. Then I'll make Breakfast.
We had sex. It was most enjoyable an animalistic twisting sweat box;
Frustrations fused; and afterwards.... ....

PREVIOUS PUBLICATIONS

L' Ephemere Review, The Blue Nib, Osiris Poetry Journal, The Ghost City Review, The High Window, A Restricted View from Under the Hedge, Picaroon Poetry Journal, Riggwelter Literary Journal, Levure Litteraire, The Arrival Magazine, Prole, The Dawntreader, The Journal, Proletarian Poetry, Rising Phoenix Review, Poets' Espresso Review, The Poetry Village, Dodging the Rain.

Other Publications

Dystopia 38.10 *(Erbacce-Press) Winner of the Erbacce Prize for Poetry 2015*
One Million Tiny Cuts *(Clare Song Birds Publishing House)*
A Season in Another World *(Thirty West Publishing House)*
The Feeding *(Rum Do Press) Venice and London (Booklet)*

TESTIMONIALS

"In Woodworm, Matt Duggan conjures "A collection of the graceful and grotesque littered streets." This book reconnoiters the landscape of contemporary society with an affectionate and skeptical glower. Part visionary, part inebriate of time and sprawl, the voice that boosts these poems over their glorious hurdles never stumbles, never quavers."

> - Tom Daley; Poet and Author, Recipient of the *Dana Award in Poetry*, *the Charles and Fanny Fay Wood Prize and* Author of *House You Cannot Reach* and *Canticles & Inventories*

"Matt Duggan casts an acerbic eye on the "world of masks" that "waits outside the door" and warns, "we are building our own prisons" in the "Post-Truth Age." Rough-tongued commentaries and haunting landscapes carry *Woodworm* into a new register that dares invoke nostalgia with a restrained and melancholy palette."

> - Andrea Moorhead; Poet & Editor of *Osiris Poetry Journal & Director of Deerfield Academy Press*

"In Woodworm Matt Duggan proves he is the natural heir to Rimbaud, Ginsberg, and O' Hara, an adept exponent of an edge that bursts wide the parameters of poetic discourse, powered by an irresistible propulsion. His work offers a refracted perspective, combining social commentary and visionary insights, informed by a fierce intelligence. This is post-modernist expressionism at its very best."

> - David Mark Williams; Poet & Author *Papaya Fantasia (Hedgehog Poetry Press) The Odd Sock Exchange (Cinnamon Press)*

"Woodworm is described as the wood-eating larvae of beetles that left unchecked cause structural damage to large buildings and small residences alike. What an apropos symbol for Matt Duggan's latest diatribe regarding planet earth slipping ever deeper into dystopian quicksand, thus, creating structural damage that leaves gaping wounds in humanity itself. A major theme throughout Duggan's book concerns how the state of innocence, that period of human curiosity and exploration, degrades into the crass sensibility of materialism and not the intelligent evolutionary path leading from innocence to wisdom via Blake's road of excess. The lexicon of Woodworm, sometimes surreal to invoke a feeling of chaos, sometimes straight forward to clarify a point, is pungent with despair concerning the lack of civility the poet now experiences in his adult life: "finger-prints are used to milk tongues in clear digital chloroform," and "Our absolute truth hangs / inside the hollow gut of a dying tree;" (the Yggdrasil tree of life). Poem after poem forlorns the insensitive beings that humans have become. One line from "The Future Isn't What We Expected," a poem detailing the despair of lost hope, sums things up: "we walk in the spaces of rented out amnesia." Innocence squandered its opportunity to evolve when callous corporations became our new trading partners: "We cut out our hearts from empathy / as repetitive nights of Kristallnacht returned. / No longer do we recognize our enemy / taking sides for the highest price." Even the solace of nature is hard to come by. While there are rare imagistic flickers positive to nature: "The morning as dark as star anise," even raw nature is tinged with suspicion regarding the banality of human intervention: "My eyes turn into giant blue turtle lights; / I watch them play in the opposite garden. / The lawn is measured and cut to exact perfection." By dividing Woodworm into the two sections, "The Pursuit of Truth" and "Questioning Sanity in a Post-Truth Age," Duggan's provocative book hints at Diogenes who has scoured the streets of humanity looking for honest men while succumbing to the grim reality of woodworms gobbling away" the foundation of humanity before our very amnesia.

- *Alan Britt, Crossing the Walt Whitman Bridge, Towson University*

"A deconstruction of modern complacency, its lexicon is deeply raw, fierce, succinct and intensely engaged with our world. As a poetic visionary he queries and warns with piercing intelligence, revealing a space of truth behind the fake frontispiece of lies we live in, I feel his new collection 'Woodworm' is the epic poem of truth our century is missing."

Maria Castro Dominguez; Poet & Writer

A Face in the Crowd (erbacce-press)

ABOUT MATT DUGGAN

Matt was born in 1971 and lives in Bristol in the U.K. with his partner Kelly and their dog Alfie, his poems have appeared in many journals across the world such as *Osiris Poetry Journal, Ink, Sweat, and Tears, The Blue Nib, Into the Void, The Journal, The Dawntreader, Midnight Lane Boutique, Anti–Heroin Chic Journal, The High Window, A Restricted View from Under the Hedge, Ghost City Review, Laldy Literary Journal, L' Ephemere Review, Carillion, Lakeview International Literary Journal, Levure Litteraire, erbacce journal, The Stray Branch, Prole, Black Light Engine Room, Militant Thistles,* Matt won the *Erbacce Prize* for Poetry in 2015 with his first full collection of poems *Dystopia 38.10* and became one of five core members at *Erbacce-Press,* where Matt interviews poets for the *erbacce-journal,* organises events and reads with the other members for the annual erbacce prize.
In 2017 Matt won the *Into the Void Poetry Prize* with his poem *Elegy for Magdalene,* and read his work across the east - coast of the U.S.A. with readings at the prestigious Cambridge Public Library Poetry Series in Boston, a guest poet appearance at The Parkside Lounge and Sip This in New York, Matt read at his first U.S. book launch in Philadelphia and has two new chapbooks available *One Million Tiny Cuts (Clare Song Birds Publishing House)* and *A Season in Another World* (*Thirty West Publishing House*) plus a small limited edition booklet *The Feeding* (Rum Do Press) Venice and London. He has read his work across the world including The Poetry on the Lake Festival in Orta, Italy, the Poetry Café in London, and in Paxos in Greece and at various venues across the U.K.